Daily dose of Happiness

Pas Simpson

Published by Motivational Press, Inc.
1777 Aurora Road
Melbourne, Florida, 32935
www.MotivationalPress.com

Manufactured in the United States of America.

ISBN: 978-1-62865-231-4

The book is dedicated to my sister Penelope "Penny" Kinight. Sometime one penny is worth more than a million dollars. To my wife and my four loving children Joshuah, Precious, Justice and Ayanna. To my my mother the person that taught me the power of belief and my Dad who taught me patience and humility can lead to great

A special thank to Leon " Herc " Baxton who was the first person outside of my family to believe in me. The Reid Family, Greg and Allyn for your guidance and support thought this process. Terri Levine for sharing a smile with me and introducing me to Justin. Last but not least Bernie Dohnrmann for entrusting me with great responsibility when others might have thought he was insane

I have been brainwashed by faith to know that I can to do it!!!

The wealthiest person is not the one that can extract most from their pockets. It is the one who can extract the most from their mind!!!

Be sure of yourself and your purpose, so that no one can shake your confidence, but anyone can lift your spirit!!!

Time is like money. Only invest it in places where it will be most appreciated and where it can do the most good!!!

Love is to do God's work because God is love!!!

Just because someone knows your name doesn't mean they know your soul. Don't let other's negative thoughts determine how you live, grow!!!

Love of life can be lost when you give too little to too much, and too much to too little. Free your mind and lead with your heart!!! Live passionately!!!

Great living is comprised of 4 words:

-1st Belief - Everything starts and ends here.

-2nd Purpose - When you know your one reason for living everyday, it will become more fulfilling.

-3rd Agenda (desired wants) - Everyone has one, including yourself. It is important to know our purpose to determine when we can match agendas.

-4th Choice - We were given free will to learn to make good choices. There is nothing more gratifying than making an informed and educated decision.

Listen with love. If a person can tell you what they are not getting, but can never express what they are not giving. It might be time to give to someone more appreciative!!!

Take charge of your life or your life will take charge of you!!!

Throw out any idea that does not serve you or interferes with your happiness when given the opportunity to serve others!!!

The only beliefs that matter are your own!!! The only actions that count are your own, the only person it really matters to is you because only you can keep you happy!!! Look in the mirror and smile!!!

Let setbacks motivate you to appreciate your successful moments more!!!

Burning desire is the fire that keeps the flame of life going!!!

Life is like a motion picture. But you must be in motion working at your dream for the picture to become 3-D!!!

God rewards the faithful and the grateful. So every great thought should be given 3 thank-you's:

-Thank you for the opportunity to be given this thought.

-Thank you for the blessings that are received from the thought coming into fruition.

-Thank you for the opportunity to bless others because of this great thought.

Never allow anyone to support your misery; however, they could assist in your happiness!!!

Be kind to yourself and walk away from the negative souls. In order to feel positive. Their bad feelings have nothing to do with you, but are a reflection of their soul!!!

You can't be everything. You can only be you!!!

There are only 2 types of people in life. Those who are pushing your dreams forward and those who are clouding your vision. People can be both. The only thing that changes is their agendas and their fears. Listen with love, so you can know what you're hearing. Counseling will help you fly, but opinion loves inactivity.

Soar!!!

You are the master of your destiny and controller of your fate. Thank God for not making you perfect, but giving you a chance everyday to be great!!!

Make sure your habits are conducive to your dreams or you will have to change dreams and/or habits to find happiness!!!

The devil is in the doubt. So believe. And educate yourself to develop a stronger belief!!!

If you never ask the question; the answer is always No!!! Live Fearlessly!!!

Dreams only become fairytales when you refuse to act on them!!!

The two most important beliefs are in God (creator) and in yourself!!!

To achieve greatness, you must first learn how to be grateful!!!

Do more, feel more, think more, and talk less!!!

Most of us search our whole lives for miracles; instead, of looking in the mirror and searching our hearts.

Become a true believer!!! There are no doubts in true believers because doubt is the absence faith. To live miraculously: be happy and grateful to be so faithful!!!

A helping hand is never afraid to ask for another helping hand!!!

Laugh instead of crying. Give unconditionally instead, of looking to receive. There is joy in all things even in loss. When we accept the blessing, we can always live a happy fulfilling life!!!

It is not your job to judge; it is our blessing to love!!!

Express love every second you can because it will impress love in your heart, forever!!!

Never take the kind words of others for granted or the mean words of others to heart!!!

-

I thank God for not making me perfect, but it always gives me something to strive for, allows me to get better every day, develops my humility, which allows me to serve more!!!

Let faith and belief lead the way, but continuous self-reflection will make sure you stay on your upward journey!!!

If you cannot lift someone's spirit, then say nothing. If someone tries to hurt you, laugh; it feels good. You were born a winner, so you can laugh in the face of the loser talk!!!

Define your truth with your heart!!!

Fair is a place to play games, enjoy the rides, and, possibly, see something unique, but it has no bearing on life. Life is never fair! More importantly, it is what you make of it and what you are willing to accept!!!

Give thanks for the things you have and haven't received. You are blessed!!!

Keeping God on your mind and in your hearts makes everyday a holiday aka holy day!!!

Embrace your fear!!! Own your failures, which make your success more rewarding!!!

●

There is too little room for growth. If you convince yourself, you are grown!!! I am growing and getting better daily, but I will never be grown, until I am gone!!!

Challenges are given to create character!!! Challenges don't make or break people, people make or break challenges!!!

Never be convinced that you can't learn something new!!!

It is not your job to judge others, but to notice how their presence affects you. If it doesn't resonate, leave. If it feels good, do good!!!

It is easy to hate, but love takes some work!!!

Celebrate all accomplishments, but enjoy every challenge!!!

Nothing is more regrettable than not asking the necessary questions to help you progress!!!

You can never feel good, if it is at the expense of others!!!

Focus and accountability are two major keys to success. Thank god for having developing control of these keys at all times. Stay focused and strive!!!

Somewhere, there is someone hating on you for no reason, but they will introduce more people to your work and they will be grateful for your efforts. Love your loved ones for their love propels you and love your hater for that love prepares and promotes you!!!

The holy trinity of success:

-1st- Believe you can do it.

-2nd- Be happy and grateful to have the opportunity to do it.

-3rd- Bless others because you are doing it.

I love me enough for all of us, so that I always have some to spare for you!!!

Free will gives us the right to choose happiness at all times. Self-education teaches us how to remain happy at all times, but it's our faith that lets us believe God created us to be happy, healthy, and wealthy!!!

Time is too precious to waste on unhappy moments. Your present is a gift and you should spend your days celebrating your life!!!

Learn to listen with your heart. It will allow you to feel the true intentions of a person instead being fooled by slick talk and jargon.

The more time you take to learn, the deeper your passion will burn!!! The more you grow, the brighter your glow. Shine. It's your time!!!

The best form of self-control is control of thought. If you do not control your thoughts, others will. Watch who and what you listen to because what you feed your mind will determine your level of control.

When you are grateful for all that you have now, you can never be mad about what you haven't received yet!!! Count your blessings, not your losses!!!

Go after what you want now. You can improve your vision along the journey.

I am humbly self-confident, not arrogant. We were born to shine!!! I never said I was better than you, you may have just felt I was. I am living proof. We can all make it!!!

Only you can determine how great today feels to you!!!

Failing is fun with a lesson attached. The level of your success will be determined by what you learned and the enjoyment you found by learning it!!!

Never be afraid to take a step back,

in order to take two steps forward!!!

God is a great comedian. When situations arise, be thankful for the challenge, and laugh as you handle it. We have a choice every time. We can laugh at the joke or become part of the joke!!!

To reach new heights, you must try new things!!!

Remain in the present because the past is gone and the future has yet to be determined. Appreciate the blessing of where you are and there will always be more blessings for you to enjoy!!!

When you live to serve others, you can dream with your eyes open!!!

Laugh when others may cry. Persevere when others may quit. Be flexible where others may break. Success is a dream fulfilled!!!

Finding strength. A lesson in every defeat will propel you to championship levels of thinking!!!

Speak with a blessed tongue and your days and hours will be continually blessed. Know and understand there's a blessing in all things, even what others may deem as a curse. The protection is in the faith!!!

Love yourself enough to love all those that want to feel love, extend love to those who may not want it, but do not let their hate invade your heart or mind!!!

Give all you can from your heart,

God will always multiply the gift, in return!!!

Confidence may come from being prepared, from being attractive, from having some knowledge, but it really should come from just being you!!!

We can say what we want, but our actions will determine the validity of our words!!!

Don't let people who give you minimal effort, make maximum demands from your life!!!

Every good leader knows who to follow!!!

When you focus and talk about the things you lack, you bring out more lacking in your life. If you focus on your blessings and appreciate the things you do have, you attract more blessings. Live happy and grateful!!!

Courage is not the absence of fear. But a realization that fear was here, but we just don't care because God walks with me!!!

Love is not a word, it is an expression, an action, an emotion (energy in motion). People will tell you they love you, but the sincere will show you that they love you. Give love unconditionally and reap love's rewards unconditionally!!!

Choose to be different and you can live differently!!!

Don't waste your gifts!!! Every second in life is a gift. That is why, no matter what time it is, we remain in the present!!!

You can never be knocked off your pedestal, if you remember to remain grounded!!! Bless-fully humble!!!

A simple smile could unlock your happiest days. Smile more genuinely and receive more honestly!!!

The only person stopping or slowing down your dream life is you. No matter who may get to enjoy the great times with you; no one will ever be able to feel exactly what your dream feels like because your dream is unique!!!

Our lives up to this point are the sum of past thoughts and beliefs. So let's make a commitment to say - I think good, I do good, I am good, so every day is a great day!!! Think it, say it, just makes sure we feel it!!!

Feed your mind better than you feed your belly. You will live a happy, healthy, and wealthy life!!!

The apostrophe T is the worst crutch to lean on because it is the crutch that crushes dreams. Replace don't, won't, and can't with do, will, and can. For instance, I do live a happy life, I will be grateful always, so I can accomplish anything I set my mind to!!!

Do not try to convince the world of your greatness, but never let anyone in the world convince you that you are not great!!!

Our thoughts are the gatekeepers to our dream life!!! Charge your thoughts with negative emotion and open the door to your living nightmares. Charge them with gratitude and positive emotions and live a blessed fantastic lifestyle!!!

Real success is like a staircase to heaven. Don't worry about the ones you miss or skip. Take time to reflect on how enjoyable your climb has been and the people you helped along the way!!!

Every chance you get scream, "I love my life," because no matter where you are in life there is someone that would be appreciative just to have those opportunities. The glory comes in the gratitude!!!

Expect the best, prepare to be blessed so you can bless others!!! Preparing for the worst means there is a doubt in your beliefs, no matter how small!!!

Stimulate your brain with good things and it will fill your life with even greater people and possessions!!!

Do not let your current reality doom your future. For things to get better, we must first feel it, visualize it, and believe in your vision enough to act. It is your God given right to live a happy life!!!

In order to reach the life of your dreams, you must fall at least once. You cannot reach new heights, if you never risk falling!!!

Doubt is a choice, so choose faith!!!

Creating you was no less miraculous than the making of heaven and earth. Understand, believe, and live remarkably!!!

When you walk in faith, you are never alone!!! We are all connected by the only thing that separates us, which is our level of belief!!! Do not miss any blessings wasting a moment in doubt. You cannot spell out testimony without going through tests!!!

Learn to appreciate yourself enough that you don't need the appreciation of others!!!

You control your thoughts and actions. Don't waste time defending them; instead, do more to be the blessing and show how blessed and highly favored you truly are!!!

Love for life and creativity turns obstacles into opportunities and more opportunities into glorious adventures!!!

People who spend time hating, lose precious time loving. Don't waste your time hating or with haters when there are so many others that want to share or can benefit from your love!!!!

Today is so much better than yesterday because yesterday is gone and today is "I can do everything," so I can enjoy many more tomorrow's!!!

We are never smart enough, learn something new every day!!!

There is no meaningful success without real sacrifice!!!

Surround yourself with people that support your voice, but never are afraid to speak the truth!!!

Action speaks louder than words. The more you act on your dreams the less time you have to hope that they will come true!!!

If you love you, so will anyone that matters!!!

Daydreaming lets you peek in the window of your happiest reality.

God made you extraordinary!!! Don't settle for less!!!

Today is the 1st day of the rest of your life. Live it to the fullest!!!

Only you can determine your worth, the world can only make suggestions!!!

It is not better to give than receive. It is better to receive enough, so you can keep giving!!!

Success is not defined by the amount of money you have, but by the number of people you help!!!

Give more heart to heart hugs, so people can feel your love and enjoy what you bring!!!

You can never be grateful and complain at the same time!!!

There is no such thing as normal. There are just some limitations that people accept!!! Live extraordinary!!!

You can teach yourself how to find the truth or learn to live accepting lies others put in front of you!!!

You don't need to think outside the box because the box never existed!!! So, now you can just think!!!

Put your haters to work!!!

Accomplish more today!!!

If you come with up with inspired thought, you owe it to yourself to follow it up with equaled action!!!

Yesterday is gone, so you must live today like there is no promise of tomorrow. Therefore, many tomorrow's can be enjoyed more than yesterday!!!

Winning is developed through habit. Losing is result of lack of discipline!!!

Your truth is a lie to anyone that does not believe it. But, it can change the life of someone that truly supports it. Live your truth!!!

Almost as important as believing in yourself is the belief in the team you are a part of.

Together,

Each

Achieves

More!!!

Leaders are still human. Don't waste time on their faults. Apply the useful information and enjoy the rest as a comedic bonus. No one is perfect, but many can teach!!!

To live blessed and highly favored, you must 1st think you are blessed. You must believe that you are blessed and then you must become the blessing!!!

Our soul never ages; it is the ultimate daydreamer and is the visionary that paints the picture of our lives. Let the soul lead and the flesh follow. You'll enjoy more of your todays and bless more people in your tomorrows!!!

Step out of your own way, so you can step into a greater you!!!

I deserve better! I will get better!! So I am Happy and Grateful to be better today than I was yesterday!!!

Confidence comes from the ability to fall on your face and just not care. You are only as good as you think you are and will only be as great as you think you can be. All good or bad accomplishments start with your thoughts about yourself!!!

Succeed, so you can inspire!!

You have nothing to prove, but so much you can do. Just do it!!!

Useless truth is still useless; nevertheless, not all knowledge is useful. Feed your need and controlled information is key to growth with speed!!!

It is not your job to change anyone's opinion of you. It is your job to know the truth about yourself and to allow the world to share your true vision!!!

You only die once, but you can be living dead; if you don't live passionately!!!!

Go. Overthinking stops real working!!!

Too many happy times are being missed due to focusing on unhappy yesterdays. Don't worry, live happy!!!

Character is built accepting challenges as blessings!!!

Live unrealistically!!! To live a life of your dreams, you can never let your current situation define your potential. God helps those who help themselves. Believe in God, have faith in your vision, and act accordingly.

Focused desire will increase the success rate of your dreams. Yearn for what you want for the right reasons and believe it can be achieved!!!

Don't let another's opinion of you ever sway your belief in God and self. As long as you and God know the real you, that is all that ever matters!!!

There is only one you, there is no competition for that. You are no better or worse than anyone; no matter how much money, knowledge, or education you may have. Love yourself, uplift others, and live a blessed life!!!

When you pay it forward, it is God who pays you back. Live charitably to lead a rewarding and fulfilling life!!!

Ignore all opinions because they are baseless, but always seek and apply the wisdom of counsel. Their words are priceless to your success!!!

Memories are what you make them out to be. They are all good: some are lessons, some are motivation, and some just tickle your soul. Own your memories, they were great and when they are over, you are in control!!! Because of them, your present is always a gift!!!

Treat people like you want to be treated. If they want to be around you, no matter how they treat you, let them come and go with love!!!

We are born with unlimited ability to give. When someone tells you they have nothing to give, then pay attention and find someone that wants to match your unlimited possibilities to be creative and give more!!!

Hey Birds. Chickens don't fly, so you better surround yourself with Eagles, if you want to soar!!!

Life gives you exactly what you think about, talk about, and focus on. Everything starts in your mind. To get more out of anything, put more into everything you care about. Excuses steal your power!!!

Dream a dream, so big it makes others want to live part of that dream with you!!!

God is within all of us, we are given a chance daily to create something, out of nothing. There is no limit to our potential, but all things take sacrifice!!! We must give to get. What negative thoughts can you give up to allow more good ones to flow in your life? Miracles happen in the mind 1st!!!

Problems do not just exist. Challenges build character, so live life like a cartoonist. Draw the life you want to live in your head first, then be happy and grateful along the way as life starts to color in between the lines for you!!!

It is never selfish to take care of your family, first. It is selfish to not be charitable whenever possible. Charity does not have to be monetary, but it must be sincere. Be a blessing to continually be blessed!!!

Accept your birthrights. A champion, who is one of a kind!!! Enjoy being you and become the best you can be because no one can be a better you!!!

Silence can be so kind!!!

Wise people learn from the mistakes of others instead, of judging them for trying. Live wealthy and wise!!!

Don't wait to say thank you until after you received the blessing; give thanks for just having the possibility to earn another blessing. The grateful reaps the greatest rewards.

Any moment you want a part of your life to be better, you must feel it's possible and believe it will be better. Thank God in advance for giving you the necessary tools to make your dream happen!!!

Life is the blessing; what you do with it is a bonus!!!

Sometimes stepping back to see people, or situations, for what they're worth is stepping forward in, so many ways!!

It's not a failure to quit something that is holding back your dreams. It is sometimes your wisest decision!!!

In order to live a miraculous life, you must start living your life in faith!!!

Don't over anything, over think, over react, over compensate, etc. Anytime you go over, you have gone too far. Remain in the moment and act from your heart.

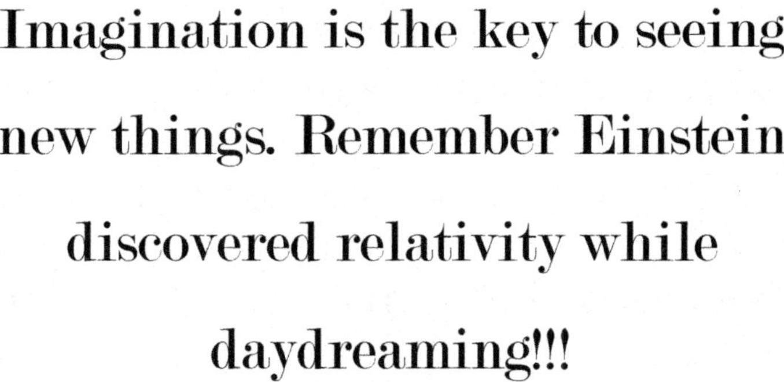

Imagination is the key to seeing new things. Remember Einstein discovered relativity while daydreaming!!!

Nothing is amazing as a clear mind. Find time to focus your mind to see your dreams all come true!!!

God loved the world so much that he gave us, you to bless and be blessed. For you to love and have faith, all dreams worked for sincerely must come true!!!

The only thing to fear is fear because with fear, there is a lack of faith!!!

Challenges are the foundation, which all character is built on!!!

1st you must feel it can happen, then you must think it will happen, but you always have to work to make it happen. There is a test in every testimony: Conceive, Believe, and Achieve!!!

Work smart, so you can soar further!!!!

3 greatest gifts:

1. Free will- You have the right to choose love.

2. Gratitude- Be happy and grateful for all love you receive even perceived setback.

3. Charity- The right to give and spread love at all times!!!

If you spend your life giving it all you have, then you will never have time to worry about what you haven't!!!

The time is always now, no matter what time of day you check it. The more you can do now, the happier you will be later!!!

A person who follows opinions can easily be lead astray, but a person who only follows counsel can climb the ladder of success, happily and gratefully!!!

Love (charity) is never really repaid by the person that receives it, but by God for you taking the time to give unconditionally is the payment. Love hard, live happy!!!

In order to reach the life of your dreams, you must fail, at least once. No risk equals no reward!!!

Living is comprised of many small things (atoms, milliseconds, family, moments, etc.) that form our big picture!!!

Spend more time focusing on the little things that make life great!!!

Don't waste time with people who only remind you of yesterday failures; enjoy life with people who focus on today's results and tomorrow's possibility!!!

Get to know yourself well enough to give the best you to the world every day!!!

Everyone has the same amount of potential, but only you can determine how much time you will spend to develop yours!!!

Do more not because you have to, not because you are paid. Do more because you are blessed to!!!

Gratitude takes practice, but you can start at any time!!!!

Discipline feels like punishment, unless it is self-imposed. Discipline yourself or be punished by the world!!!

Time is more valuable than money.

Make sure you invest it in the places,

where it will appreciate most.

Listen with love. If a person can tell you what they are not getting, but can never express what they are not giving. It might be time to give to someone more appreciative!!!

Learn to appreciate yourself enough that you don't need the appreciation of others to justify your unlimited giving. Yet, develop the awareness to give to the grateful, so they can continue to pass on the gifts!!!

Be sure of yourself and your purpose, so that no one can shake your confidence, but anyone can lift your spirit!!!

Do not waste time trying to explain who you are. Be laser focused on your purpose, execute, spread love and your actions, and the world will talk for you!!!

Misery loves company, but so does happiness. Choose wisely!!!

Love for life and creativity turns obstacles into opportunities and opportunities into glorious adventures!!!

Follow your feelings. Feel good to do great!!!

To be a perfectionist, sets yourself up for consistent failure because nothing is ever perfect. Always give your best, which allows for you to enjoy success while leaving room for improvement!!!

If you only address what you need, you will never get what you want!!!

If you pay it forward, God (universe) pays you back, exponentially!!!

The successful person is usually not afraid to learn from their repeated failures!!!

To achieve greatness, you must first learn how to be grateful!!!

We were born with free will. So, we have the right to choose to be happy, healthy, and wealthy. Make the choice to be your greatest you, every day!!!

Reading is freedom and a key to unlocking your happiest self because to read is to discover for yourself and to learn is to think, critically. If we don't read, we remain slaves to the words of the people we meet or know!!!

Love yourself enough that you will never miss a second of love, let it overflow, so you can express, spread, and give love every day!!!

True confidence does not come from feeling superior to others. True confidence comes from being comfortable being you, knowing you are prepared, and are ready to serve others!!!

A simple smile can be the gateway to happier times. Smile like the favored child you are!!!

You do not need to know how you are going to accomplish your goal; you just need to have a big enough WHY to see it to the end!!!

Even when you are down, you are not out until you stop believing!!!

The most important thing in the world is family.

Parts of your family,

you are born into and others,

come through love and mutual respect, both are equally important.

Family 1st!!!

Others may try to cripple the body, but only you can cripple your mind and the soul!!!

A wish will always remain a wish, until you add some emotion to form desire: unwavering gratitude for it being possible and persistent action for it ever to become real!!!

The best lesson in life is everything you in need starts with self: self-confidence, self-education, self-love, self-starter, self-reliant, etc. except humility. Being humble enough to always say "thank you" for being blessed and ability, in turn, become a blessing.

There is no such thing as spare time or free time: there is just time. You can use it towards your dreams or let it pass towards your nightmares. It is always your time!!!

Learn to appreciate yourself enough that you don't need the appreciation of others, so they can continue to pass on the gifts!!!

Share your story (testimony) with love, don't waste time convincing spectators, but enjoy every moment you can with the participators!!!

Answers with no solutions is wasted energy, with no focus!!!

Practice what you at teach. The only time people like to be preached to is when you are behind the pulpit and even then you might get tuned out!!!

I am no better nor worse than you. I am just here to help or be helped, so I can become more helpful!!!

Create the type of life you want live, instead a life you are always looking to vacate from!!!

Replace stressing with feel the blessing, replace delaying with more praying, and replace judging with loving. Secrets to the Happiest Self!!!

Thank a hater their presence: lets you know that you are on the right track and don't diminish their value!!!

When you sincerely want to serve, you can only laugh and enjoy the way God (universe) put the people in place to help you serve more!!!

If you do and say everything from your heart, you will never mind!!!

Give from your soul

and the blessing will flow!!!

A thought is the most powerful thing known to man. A thought could make you healthy or make you sick. A simple thought could cripple you, or drive you crazy, or it can empower you to change the lives of entire generation. The wealthy and healthy learn to train and control their thoughts, while the sick and poor allow their thoughts to control them. The only way to have self-control is to control what, why, and how you think about things!!!

The things in life you regret are not the things you did to make you who you are, but the things you didn't do to become who you wanted to be!!!

Surround yourself with people and activities that can help you work to be your best.

I love you even if you don't love me because I can and God will bless me for it!!!

To become the greatest you, you cannot be afraid to let go your worst parts. Take more time to be honest with yourself, improve yourself, and the world around will improve with it. The most fulfilling work we can ever do is the work we do on ourselves!!!

We are blessed to have been made in the image of the creator. To fully receive that blessing and fulfill our purpose, we must create. All creation starts with thought and the best thoughts start by giving gratitude and glory to God!!!

Life doesn't give us what we want. It gives us what we think. Stay focused on love, gratitude, and abundance. The grateful receive that grace!!!

Take the time to respect and appreciate the little things, it will allow the big things to be that more enjoyable!!!

Being grown up doesn't mean you stop dreaming, it means you have learned how to make some dreams come true. Dream bigger!!!

The only obstacle that ever matters is you. Embrace your short comings and go further in life!!!

All things done from the heart is success!!!

If you believe in something, strongly, you must take action!!!

There is always someone telling the world who you are because they are not who they are versus who they want to be!!! Be you and be happy!!

You control your thoughts and actions, do not waste time defending them; instead, do more to be the blessing and show how blessed and highly favored you truly are!!!

You have nothing to prove, but so much potential to do. Do all you can, which will be proof in itself!!!

Feeling stressed is a choice just like feeling blessed, but only one feeling is good for your soul!!!

When others doubt, you go harder and the cavalry is on their way, but you have to have enough fight in you to be helped along the journey!!!

You can lie to yourself to make you feel good or you can tell yourself the truth to make sure you do good!!!

Every time you are given an opportunity to show what you are made of: Shine!!!

You can live the life of your dreams or become victim to everyone's nightmare!!!

You are only as strong as your beliefs!!!

To develop self-control is the greatest choice anyone can make because it frees us from being controlled by others!!!

You can never force anyone to spend their life with you, but you can enjoy any time they had to give!!!

Let the doubters doubt and the haters hate: it will all work out in your favor when you labor in love and faith!!!

The only devil you need to fight is the one that runs through your mind!!!

No one can shake my self-confidence because I own it. No one can lower my self-esteem because I own it, but anyone can teach me a lesson, lift my spirit, or make me laugh!!!

Never be afraid to ask for what you need. The possibilities are endless, but they answer is always "No," if you never ask!!!

Just because you have a right to doesn't always mean that you should!!!

Good things don't come easy, but they feel great when you earned them!!!

Believe when everyone else stops and win like no one else can!!!

Put pure faith into your dreams and great work ethic into your passion to live, when others can only fantasize about!!!

Never allow someone's limited view hander you limit on your expectations!!!

Whenever there is a chance to reach far, go further!!!

Don't lose because you choose to win.

You get what you desire most because

u want to win it!!!

Just because others can't see it, doesn't mean you should limit your true vision. Living your dream will help others find theirs!!!

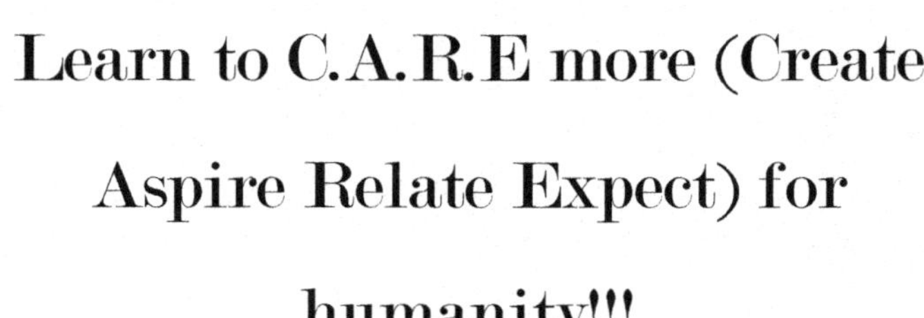

Learn to C.A.R.E more (Create Aspire Relate Expect) for humanity!!!

Fall forward towards Faith or lay down towards misery!!!

Expect challenges as proof that growth is still possible!!!

When you expect to win, prepare to win, and when you are willing to learn from setbacks, you eventually will win!!!

The greater you, that's inside, is just waiting to accept that it's there!!!

There are no ups and downs: there is only growth or acceptance!!!

You have to let go of something, in order to hold on tightly to others!!!

Be infectious or become infected!!!

Everyone makes mistakes, but only you can control how many times you make the same ones. Correct, smile, and move on. Your engineering happiness that way!!!

It's not about those "but" thoughts that allows you to do you!!!

Noticing danger and accepting fear is not one and the same. Noticing danger may save your life, but accepting fear will kill your spirit!!!

It is easy to make life hard, but it takes work to make life easy!!!

Opinions are like Assholes. Everyone has one, but only shit comes from it!!!

Enjoy every moment because you own it!!

Celebrate your accomplishments, but enjoy every challenge!!!

God gives us just what we earn in gratitude: never what we expect with complaints!!!

You can never motivate everyone to be great, but you can inspire anyone to do great!!!

The more you focus on giving: the greater receiving feels!!!

When your life is in a certain way,
be grateful. You can get excited about
every moment of the day!!!

If you accept a doubt, there will always be a reason to complain; however, if you choose faith then there will always be a reason for gratitude!!!

Be more appreciative, so that your lifestyle can appreciate!!!

Enjoy your greatness and the creator within humbleness!!!

Dreams become clearer, the more you work on them!!!

To get where you want to go, you must work with faith: living now in the know!!!

Don't wait for one special day to give: give any and every time you can from the heart. That makes every day special!!!

There are many ways to attack the world. You can stand alone like a finger or join forces like a fist: remember it's much harder to break with your fist than your finger!!! In this fight for our dreams, how many fists can you become a part of?

Define your truth with your heart!!!

The only true form of self-control is control of thought. If you don't control your thoughts, others will. Watch who and what you listen to because what you feed your mind, which will determine your level of control!!!

Believe, your greatest self is waiting on the other side!!!

Only your heart can fix what your mind has tricked!!!

Lead with love or leave with disappointment!!!

The only thing stopping you from winning is your determination. Live inspired!!!

How you feel about yourself will determine what the world thinks about you. Love yourself unconditionally!!!

You can either be awake or you can be awaken: the difference is your level of gratitude!!!

The more you intentionally feed your mind, the less time it will have for mental junk food and the healthier your thoughts will be!!!

Don't let someone negative invade your positive thoughts; instead, let your positive thoughts overcome their negative being!!!

Work on your dream like your happiest self depended on it. It does!!!

Listen to the intent of the conversation, watch the intention in every action, and it will tell you far more than the words they are saying and reveal their true nature!!!

What you fear or have faith in will develop, according to what you believe in most!!!

Intuition is just inspiration from the soul. Follow your intuitions to a happier life!!!

You never reach new horizons holding on to old fears. There are always something to let go in order to grow!!!

Love your enemy not for their sake,

but for yours!!!!

You will control every situation when you control your mind and your thoughts!!!

Life is your teacher. It just uses people and circumstances to make you better understand!!!

Feel, think, act!!! Rinse and repeat your way to wealth!!!

You were born a winner. You just need to remember why you have already won!!!

When you focus on greatness, the worst you can get is a little goodness!!!

Build your faith more than you build your muscles because faith will always make you stronger than looks!!!

If you work for love, then any monetary payment is just a bonus!!!

The way you feel about life will determine the way life treats you!!!

If you are going to wear anything, wear a smile. It is the only thing you can wear that will never go out of style!!!

Now is always the time to give your best effort!!!

Give your best in everything you do and get the best out of everything that is done!!!

What people say about you means nothing, but what people do for you should mean the world!!!

Let your clear intentions motivate others to be as great!!!!

Heaven is the most beautiful state of mind. Live heavenly!!!

The more inspired actions you can take, the more fulfilling life will become!!!

The educated man is not the person who reads the most books, but the person who can apply more of the knowledge they have received!!!

God broke the mold making you: it is up to you to remember why!!!

You can make life happen or let life happen. Either way it is going to happen, but what you do to make it happen will determine how happy you are with the results!!!

Be inspired by the doubts of others,

but never doubt yourself!!!

We are always creating. Either the life we want through gratitude or the life we don't want through complaints!!!

There is no competition for me. I am inspired by everyone and everything!!!

Arguments are a waste of time and energy. It is better to be kind than be right!!!

You just need to know where you are going and why you are going, how to get there will be figured out along the journey!!!

Laugh everyday: it is good for the soul!!!

You are only as good as what you willing to work to become a better you!!!

You succeeded the moment you thought the idea; however, your actions will determine what level of success you will enjoy!!!

The way you treat others is a reflection of how you treat yourself!!!

Adversity is the adversary, or enemy, of the weak!!!

Strength is not determined by the size of your muscles, but by the spirit of your conviction!!!

It is easy to doubt, but it takes work to develop true faith!!!

Words are powerful; therefore, be careful of what you wish for, you might just get it!!!

Your dream is yours alone, yet we all have character that play significant roles, but none more important than yours!!!

Be the most positive force in the room because everyone will gravitate to you!!!

If you are going to doubt anything, doubt the doubt because your faith is worth it!!!

You can accept the challenge or accept the defeat, but you cannot do both!!!

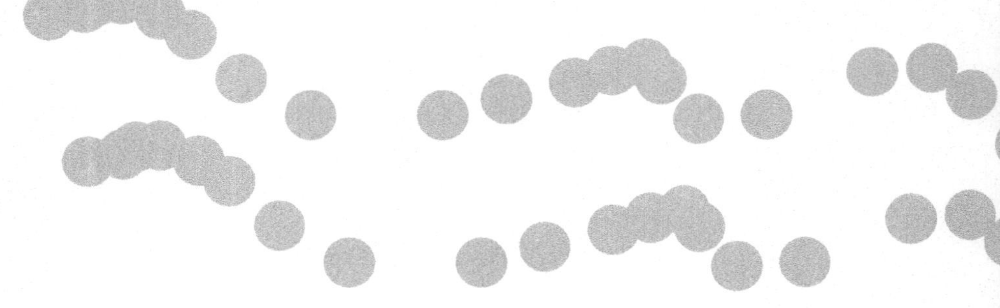

If you stay ready, you don't ever have to get ready!!!

You can never fail giving it all you have!!!

The truth is personal. Learn your truth or spend a lifetime accepting other's lies!!!

Success is a journey: you can never be mad when someone wants to get off on their stop!!!

The greatest things come when you add a little pressure. Turn you coal filled complaints into diamond shaped dreams!!!

Serve the world genuinely and the world will give to you, earnestly!!!

Honesty is the only policy that ever counts!!!

If you pray to be a blessing, you can only be blessed!!!

All things are figured out with faith, but more things are destroyed with doubt!!!

Fear is praying, in reverse!!!

There is a superhero inside all of us!!!

There is no failure in falling. Fall as many times as you need to soar!!!

Your happiest life is determined: by the lies you no longer accept, and the truths you took time to learn!!!

Meditation is key

to finding your truth!!!

Flow can never come through force. Give thanks in advance and believe. Be- (all you can) leave (it's up to your passionate work to appear)!!!

When you truly desire for the best,

you can prepare for even better!!!

Life is for living!!! The more useless tv you watch, the more envious you become over how others live. Live life or spend it watching others enjoy theirs!!!

Growth is filled with love and hate. The people that love you will give to your cause; however, if one allows haters, it can work for you. Haters are a free marketing and promotions department looking for work. Embrace all that love you, but take time to thank the spectators that will detail your progress for the world to watch you grow!!!

Don't waste time trying to change someone else's beliefs about you. Believe in yourself, so the rest of the world can believe in you, too!!!

The decision to be indecisive will hurt more than deciding and failing. Happily move forward!!!

Be a great teammate! A humble person, who helps put the "I" in "win," is not the one accepting Laughable Opinions Swooping In Negating Gratitude (LOSING). Success is a collective thing. If you don't have a good team, build one or join one based on tangible beliefs. Together Each Achieves More (TEAM)!!!

Stagnation keeps you guessing.

Decision takes massive action!!!

To live your dream life, you must go for it, without any regrets!!!

Simple math on life: Self-education + prayer + meditation + action= elevation from the plantation!!!

A simple thought can change the forces of destiny!!!

Confidence doesn't come from feeling superior to others, but from being prepared that your presence is valuable!!!!

Crunch time is my party!!!

When someone show you their ass, it is up to you whether you are going to kiss it or kick it!!!

Love yourself, so that you can truly love others!!!

Anything done with sincerity is already success!!!

A dream life is formed through insight, never eyesight!!!

I love me. I am worthy. Some people may not like me, but I don't care because the ones that matter will be glad that I am here!!!

Bonus

Being committed to your dreams is not the same as being interested in your fantasy!!!

CPSIA information can be obtained at www.ICGtesting.com
Printed in the USA
LVOW04s1222170915

454580LV00016B/187/P

9 781628 652314